LET'S PREPARE A SPEECH

8 Steps to prepare an effective speech

MUFTI AHMAD

"Speech is the mirror of the soul; as a man speaks, so is he."
Publilius Syrus

Contents

Preface

Speaking is a difficult technique, but preparing a speech is an even more difficult art.

There are hardly ten percent of speakers in the world who deliver a technically sound speech

This book provides such simple, concise and common-sense methods of speech preparation that one can prepare an excellent speech on any difficult to difficult topic in a very short time.

I can definitely say that if you want to give a speech somewhere but suffer from anxiety, hesitation and depression due to lack of proper preparation, then this book is for you.

I sincerely hope that after reading this book you will be able to prepare an excellent speech on any topic in a short period of time.

1. Getting free to prepare a speech

In arrange to perform any errand successfully, it is critical that you just allow full consideration to that assignment for a few time and take off aside other exercises, since in the event that you attempt to perform a few things at the same time, None of these assignments can be exhausted a great way since the consideration of the individual keeps changing once more and once more, due to which not as it were no assignment can be completed, but moreover the individual gets exceptionally tired and does not do anything for a few time and Will not be able to work more.

In the same way, if you want to prepare a speech or lecture on any important topic, set a day or time for it, then leave all other engagements, if possible, separate somewhere and focus your attention on that.

Fair as the human intellect is exceptionally sharp, important, endless and capable, within the same way it gets to be moderate, frail and contract. In the event that it is locked in in numerous other things whereas performing the head, at that point it embraces other properties

Therefore, if you want to prepare a subject well, then the first step is to separate yourself from all other activities for some time and devote yourself only to the preparation of this work.

2. Define your Purpose and audience

It is very important what topic you want to talk about because the speech will not be well prepared until the topic is chosen.

For a speech to be effective, it must have a clear goal. A goal also helps you focus while creating the speech.

Ask yourself: do you mainly want to…

- ❖ Entertain?

- ❖ Inform?

- ❖ Persuade?

- ❖ Motivate?

- ❖ Inspire?

Note: these goals may overlap, and one does not exclude another. But one must be your main goal.

After choosing a topic, you wish to identify the audience In order to put through together with your group of onlookers amid discourses, it is critical to be able to put yourself in their shoes. As it were from this viewpoint can you really communicate understanding and build up affinity.

To know your audience is to engage your audience.

The **Empathy Map** is a handy technique from the world of user experience and marketing, where it is used to better understand potential or existing customers. It works remarkably well when you prepare a speech, too.

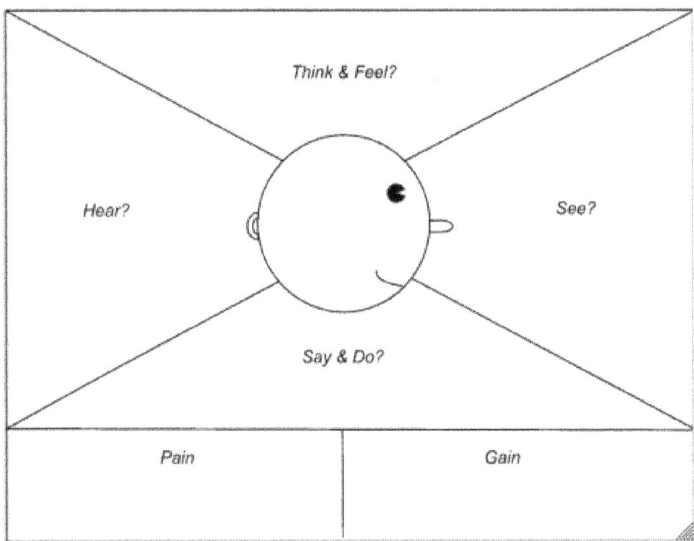

The empathy map helps you better understand your audience.

The big idea is to go over the different areas in the map and come up with the elements that create your listeners' mental world in relation to the topic.

Suppose you are to deliver a speech on the use of sugar in processed foods. Some questions the empathy map would trigger are:

- ❖ What do they think about the use of sugar and how does it make them feel?

- ❖ What do they hear about sugar from their environment or in the news?

- ❖ What do they see when it comes to sugar, e.g. in terms of advertising or packaging?

- ❖ What do they say about sugar to their peers? What do they do – what actions do they take (or not take)?

- ❖ What pain, or significant disadvantages, do they associate with sugar?

- ❖ What gain, or significant advantages, do they associate with sugar?

Note that the answers to some of these questions will overlap. Don't worry about that — this is just a brainstorming tool to trigger relevant information stored in your memory.

The point is not to organize information in any neat way.

Try it, even if it's for 5 minutes! You'll be surprised how helpful the answers are for:

- ❖ finding an angle

- ❖ finding the right words

- ❖ creating goodwill

- ❖ overcoming resistance

- ❖ and much more.

3. Start gathering materials

Conduct thorough research on your chosen topic. Utilize reputable sources such as books, articles, academic journals, and credible websites.

Take notes and compile relevant information, statistics, examples, and quotes that support your main points.

And also one thing more keep in your mind that no single person is perfect, his thoughts and actions cannot be a certificate of complete completion of any work. To complete and perfect any work, he needs the opinion, advice and help of others.

Similarly, prepare some topics on your own on the topic you want to lecture, but take feedback from your sincere friends and experts in the field. Share it with them. This tool will help you prepare your speech accurately and on topic.

Note: At this point, keep in mind that you must exchange information with seniors in the field on which you are preparing a speech.

This will help you a lot in preparing a complete outline of your speech

4. Organize Your Speech Structure and add significance

Create a clear and logical structure for your speech. Typically, a speech consists of three main parts: introduction, body, and conclusion.

In the introduction, grab the audience's attention, provide an overview of your topic, and state your thesis or main message.

In the body, organize your content into main points and sub points. Use transitions to guide your audience smoothly between ideas.

In the conclusion, summarize your key points, restate your thesis, and leave the audience with a memorable closing statement or call to action.

Important of Significance:

Crafting any good story starts with the why. What's the point exactly?

There's a saying in public speaking: you win the heart before you win the mind. Knowing the why of your speech is essential in accomplishing that.

Speakers engage an audience: by being significant; by creating meaning. Audiences feel engaged when they have the feeling the talk is also about them. A great example is Martin Luther King's famous 'I have a dream' speech. The audience did not come to see Martin Luther King, they came because they identified with his ideas. They felt his speech was about them, their lives, and their dreams.

That explains the importance of step 2: Know your audience. You can only add significance if you have a clear image of the receiving end of your speech.

How to find your speech's significance

To find the significance of your speech, ask yourself the following questions when you prepare a speech:

- ❖ Why the speech is being made?

- ❖ What do I believe, that I want to share? What do I stand for?

- ❖ So what?! Why should my audience care?

Develop Supporting Material:

Use your research findings to provide evidence, examples, anecdotes, and visuals (if applicable) that bolster your main points.

Ensure your supporting material is relevant, credible, and effectively conveys your message.

Note: It is very important here that you have to set the speech material according to the time, place and audience.

Using common words for educated people is not appropriate, similarly using deep and difficult words for common people will reduce your value.

5. Define your clear message

Today, people are flooded with information. There is an image circulating on the web which goes so far to say that a person today receives more information in a day than a person in the middle ages in his entire life!

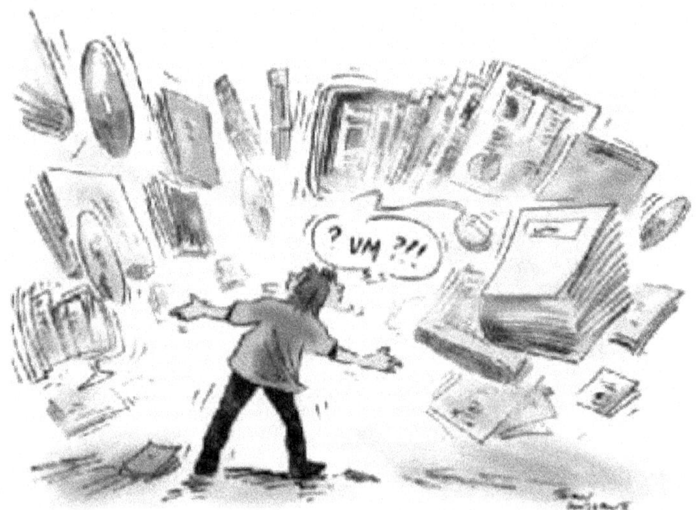

Today a person is subjected to more new information in a day than a person in the middle ages in his entire life!

True or not, we can all agree that in a device-rich world, the information intake has never been more intense.

How does that translate to speeching? Well: to make your speech memorable, I suggest you focus on extracting one key message.

Your key message should be as simple as possible, regardless of the complexity of the issues and topics at hand. It will consist of one or two phrases that express your main point.

If that sounds daunting, let's look at a model that can help.

The Message House model is a time-tested PR tool to condense complex stories into a thematic 'house'. This house is made of a set of three messages that together form the overarching key message (called the Umbrella Statement in the model).

The Core Messages on the second level represent your Umbrella Statement, but in greater detail. They can be supporting arguments, sequential steps to take, conditional statements, descriptive (think: who, what, where, when, why and how), or of another kind.

Finally, the lower part of the house provides evidence, proof points and support. This is the foundation of your story.

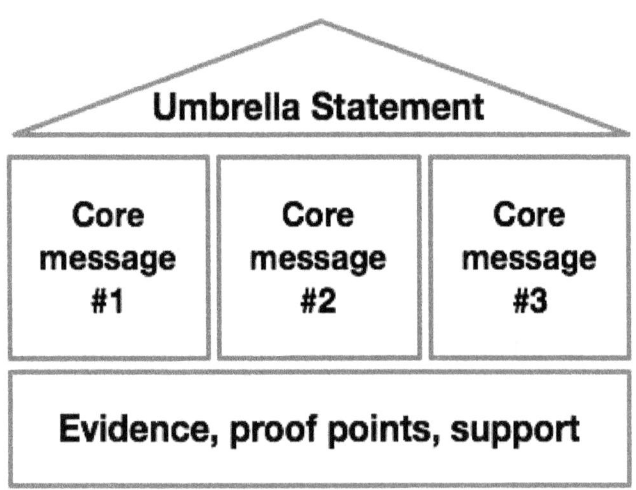

How to use the Message House

In some cases, your Umbrella Statement (that's your key message) will be very clear to you. If that's so, it's useful to come up with the 3 Core Messages that make up the Umbrella Statement.

At other times, you'll have 2 or 3 messages in mind as you prepare a speech. In that case, consider those your Core messages and start to look for the single Umbrella Statement.

Examples of Umbrella Statements and their Core Messages

1. We need to allow our employees to do more remote working.

- ❖ Employees lose time and energy along the way

- ❖ Some employees report they feel less productive in larger office spaces.

- ❖ Candidates for jobs that are hard to fill, are not attracted to our current policy.

2. We're going to paint all of the street side walls of our shops bright yellow.

- ❖ First I have to put the idea of working time and required amount and share it in the annual meeting

- ❖ Then, I will have the team communicate the exact steps to each shop owner.

- ❖ Finally, our sales representatives will check each shop they visit.

3. We've generated the most profit in the history of our company.

- ❖ Our London and Birmingham staff worked very hard

- ❖ Sales were high in December and January

- ❖ The sale of green colored heavy bikes made huge profits

6. Establish your structure

The way you organize information is essential if you want your audience to follow and understand your speech. Ideas must be put together in an orderly manner.

I therefore recommend every speaker to use an outline as the backbone for their speech.

An outline is simply 10,000 feet view of your speech. It's as if you would zoom out completely and see the major turns your speech takes.

Why use an outline?

That's easy: our brains are simply not capable of creating quality content from beginning to end.

Compare it to cooking a meal. Imagine yourself standing in front of different foods.

Without thinking ahead, you grab a couple of ingredients and start cutting, cleaning and preparing them.

Unless you're an experienced chef, that won't result in a remarkable meal, will it? Without a gameplan to prepare a speech, the end result of your creation will be underwhelming.

Here are a few general directions your outlines can take. These are based on effective storytelling principles:

- ❖ Problem – pathway – solution

- ❖ Problem – solution – reasoning

- ❖ Situation – complication – solution

- ❖ Past – present – future

After you've decided on the general direction, flesh out your outline. See if you can describe your speech in ten to fifteen bullets. Refer to your Message House (see previous point) to make sure your outline includes your Core messages.

What structure works best for your purpose? Do you have a preference? Try a few structures for your speeches and choose the one that is most persuading.

Next, integrate even more storytelling. Your bigger picture might be represented by a story, but can you integrate 'mini-stories' to illustrate specific points?

7. Prepare a strong opening and strong ending

Scientific research shows it again and again. If you ask people to rate a certain experience they had recently, they will base a lot of their opinion on how it began and how it ends. Looking back at an experience, whatever happens in the middle seems to carry less weight for us.

A classic example is a visit to a restaurant. Smart restaurant owners focus extra on doing two things impeccably: the welcoming and the dessert. Although they pay great attention to the overall experience, of course, they know that a sloppy greeting of their guests, or a below-standard dessert, can easily spoil their guests' memory of the whole evening.

For you, it means it's smart to think twice about how you open and how you close.

Ideas for a strong opening

Here are a few angles to inspire you in crafting your opening:

1. 'Start with a bang': use a quote, bold claim or striking fact, or ask a question.

2. 'So what?': Go straight to the point and open with why your audience should care.

3. 'Introduce yourself': But do it in a compelling way. Tell a juicy story. What would the tabloids write about you?

4. Make the purpose clear – What impact do you want to achieve?

Ideas for a memorable ending

1. Repeat your Key Message. Think 'key takeaway'. This is a natural-feeling and effective way to make a firm point.

2. Refer to the beginning. Most good stories develop in a circular way. A problem introduced in the beginning gets solved in the end. Balance gets restored; etcetera.

3. Present a call-to-action. If you want your audience to take a certain action, always end with that.

8. Rehearse and Refine:

Practice your speech multiple times to become comfortable with the material and your delivery.

Pay attention to your tone, pace, gestures, and body language. Make sure your voice is clear and your presence engaging.

Seek feedback from trusted individuals, such as friends, family, or colleagues, to improve your speech.

Time yourself to ensure you stay within your allotted speaking time.

Some point for Rehearse

Below are some points to practice which will improve your speech:

1. Write out, practice and tweak (optional)

At this point, you could write out your speech in full text – if you have the time.

Read your text out loud for a few times until you're comfortable with the content. You will probably still tweak a few parts.

If you don't have the time, or you feel comfortable working with just bullet points, feel free to skip to step 2!

I do highly recommend you write out your opening and ending.

2. Bring back to bullet points and practice again

Once on stage, you don't want to hold the full text of your speech in your hand. You will be tempted to look at it often, which will break your connection with the audience.

So now, reduce your text to a list of main points, keywords, facts and anecdotes. And practice your speech again. Refer back your outline from step 5 for the general structure.

This will also help you memorise the speech completely by heart faster.

Do I have to know my whole speech by heart, you ask?

My answer is: not necessarily. But as just mentioned, do know your opening and ending from the inside out.

3. Take your practice to the next level

Here are my rehearsing tips for the best results:

- ❖ Record yourself. Most beginning speakers find this tough, but it's an essential way of spotting weaknesses in your speaking and improving them.

❖ Practice for real people. The gap between practising in front of a mirror and practising in front of a crowd is just too large. Practice for a small group of colleagues or family members to get used to the stress that comes with having an audience.

❖ Ask for specific feedback. If you practice in front of people, help them evaluate you by asking them specific questions. It could be the content, your body language, or your opening. Anything you feel you need feedback on.

❖ Rehearse often. Once you're happy with your speech's content and your performance, practice your speech ten times – if you have that luxury of time. If you need more practice, go for it. There's no better confidence booster as knowing you've rehearsed your speech until it hurt 🤕